MASTERING SAS PROGRAMMING: A COMPREHENSIVE GUIDE FOR DATA ANALYSIS AND REPORTING.

DR ASHOK JAHAGIRDAR

Contents

Foreword   *v*

1. Introduction To SAS Programming   1

2. Working With Data In SAS   8

3. Advanced Data Manipulation Techniques   16

4. Statistical Analysis And Reporting In SAS   20

5. Time Series Analysis And Forecasting In SAS   29

Epilogue   45

Foreword

Welcome to **Mastering SAS Programming: A Comprehensive Guide for Data Analysis and Reporting**. This book is designed for anyone who wants to harness the power of SAS, whether you are a beginner looking to learn the basics of programming and data management or an experienced professional seeking to refine your skills and explore advanced techniques.

SAS (Statistical Analysis System) is a powerful and versatile software suite widely used for data manipulation, statistical analysis, and reporting across a variety of industries, including healthcare, finance, academia, and government. Its ability to handle large datasets, perform complex statistical calculations, and generate detailed reports makes it an essential tool for data analysts, statisticians, and business professionals alike.

The objective of this book is to guide you through the entire spectrum of SAS programming, from foundational concepts to advanced topics. We start by introducing the core elements of SAS, such as data structures, syntax, and basic procedures. As you progress through the chapters, you will delve into more complex subjects like macro programming, statistical modeling, and time series analysis. We also emphasize the practical aspects of reporting and automation, equipping you with the tools to create efficient, reusable code for real-world applications.

Throughout the book, you'll find hands-on examples, detailed explanations, and practical tips designed to help you build a deep understanding of SAS programming. Whether you are performing routine data management tasks or tackling advanced statistical analysis, this guide provides you with the knowledge and techniques necessary to master SAS.

I encourage you to experiment with the examples, adapt the techniques to your own projects, and continuously explore the capabilities of SAS. By the time you finish this book, you will be equipped with a comprehensive skillset that will empower you to tackle any data analysis or reporting challenge with confidence.

I hope this book serves as a valuable resource on your journey to mastering SAS programming, and I look forward to seeing how you apply the techniques and concepts covered within to solve complex problems and unlock new insights from your data.

Happy coding!

Dr Ashok Jahagirdar

PhD (Information Technology)

CHAPTER ONE

Introduction to SAS Programming

What is SAS

SAS, an abbreviation for **Statistical Analysis System**, is a comprehensive software suite developed by the SAS Institute.

It is used in various industries, including finance, healthcare, education, and government, to perform tasks such as data management, advanced analytics, business intelligence, and predictive modeling.

The software's main strength lies in its ability to handle large datasets, perform complex statistical analyses, and generate clear, detailed reports.

SAS provides tools for:

- **Data Entry, Retrieval, and Management:**
- from simple data manipulation to working with large-scale databases.
- **Statistical Analysis:**
- from descriptive statistics to complex modeling.
- **Report Generation:**
- SAS can produce detailed reports, charts, and graphs for clear data interpretation.

- **Data Mining and Predictive Analytics**:
- Using machine learning algorithms to discover patterns and trends in data.

- Why Learn SAS?

SAS is a dominant player in the data analysis and statistics world,

- particularly in industries like
- pharmaceuticals,
- banking, and
- government agencies, where
- security,
- scalability, and
- regulatory compliance are critical.

Learning SAS can provide significant advantages:

- **Industry Standard**:

SAS is widely used in industries requiring high accuracy and regulatory compliance, such as clinical trials, financial risk management, and government statistics.

- **Scalability**:

SAS can handle datasets that are terabytes in size without performance degradation.

- **Comprehensive Suite**:

SAS is more than just a programming tool; it offers complete solutions for reporting, analytics, and data visualization.

- **Job Market**:

Many companies continue to rely on SAS, and proficiency in it opens up career opportunities in analytics, research, and reporting roles.

SAS has also evolved to work alongside open-source tools like Python and R, making it more versatile in the current data science landscape.

- Core Components of SAS

SAS consists of various modules that allow users to perform different types of data manipulation, analysis, and reporting tasks. Some of the key components are:

- **Base SAS**: This is the core of SAS, used for data entry, management, and basic statistical procedures.
- **SAS/STAT**: A collection of advanced statistical tools used for hypothesis testing, linear regression, and multivariate analysis.
- **SAS/GRAPH**: Tools to create detailed and customizable charts, graphs, and visualizations.
- **SAS/ETS**: Used for econometrics and time series analysis, vital for financial forecasting and modeling.
- **SAS/ACCESS**: Facilitates access to external databases such as Oracle, MySQL, and SQL Server, allowing seamless integration with other data sources.
- **SAS Enterprise Guide**: A graphical user interface (GUI) that allows users to access the power of SAS without needing to write code. It's particularly useful for non-programmers to execute SAS tasks.
- **SAS Viya**: A modern, cloud-enabled platform that integrates advanced analytics, machine learning, and

data visualization, allowing faster and more efficient data processing and analysis.

- SAS Programming Language Basics

The SAS programming language consists of statements and steps used to manipulate data, perform analyses, and produce output. At the core of SAS programming are two types of steps:

- **DATA Step**: Used for data manipulation such as reading in data, filtering, merging datasets, creating new variables, and applying transformations.
- **PROC Step**: Short for **Procedure**, the PROC step calls SAS's vast library of procedures to perform various types of analyses, statistical calculations, and report generation.

Example of a SAS program:

```
data mydata;
input Name $ Age Gender $;
datalines;
John 25 M
Alice 30 F
Bob 22 M
;
run;
proc print data=mydata;
run;
```

In this example:

- **DATA Step**: Reads in a dataset containing Name, Age, and Gender.
- **PROC Step**: Prints the dataset to the output window.

- How SAS Executes a Program

SAS follows a sequential execution model. It processes each step of the program in the order it is written. SAS programs consist of statements that are terminated by a semicolon (;), and execution occurs in two main phases:

1. **Compilation Phase:**

SAS reads the program code, checks for syntax errors, and prepares to execute the code.

2. Execution Phase:

SAS executes the compiled code, either manipulating data in a DATA step or performing an analysis using a PROC step.

- SAS Programming Environment

SAS offers several different environments for writing and executing code:

- SAS Studio:

A web-based interface that allows users to write and run SAS code without installing any software locally. It's accessible from any web browser and is particularly useful for cloud-based deployments.

- SAS Enterprise Guide:

A GUI-based interface where users can create projects, use process flows, and run code snippets.

- SAS Display Manager System (DMS):

The traditional interface with an Editor Window for writing code, a Log Window for error messages, and an Output Window to view results.

Each of these environments has its pros and cons, but SAS Studio and SAS Enterprise Guide are the most commonly used in modern SAS workflows.

- Understanding the SAS Log and Output

The **SAS Log** is crucial for debugging and ensuring the correctness of a program.

The log provides detailed information about the execution of each step in the program, including:

- Errors (e.g., syntax errors or data-related issues).
- Warnings (e.g., potential issues that do not stop the program).
- Notes (e.g., summary information about the execution, such as the number of observations read).

The **Output Window** or **Results Viewer** displays the results of the analyses performed by PROC steps, which can include tables, charts, and summary statistics. Clear understanding of the log is essential for debugging and improving code.

- **Key SAS Syntax Rules**
- **Case Insensitivity**:

SAS is not case-sensitive, meaning data, DATA, and Data are treated the same.

- **Statement Termination**:

Every statement must end with a semicolon (;).

- **Comments**: You can add comments using either /* Comment */ for block comments or * Comment; for single-line comments.

Example of using comments in SAS:
```
/* This is a block comment */
data employees;
input Name $ Age Salary;
```

```
/* This is a comment explaining the datalines */
datalines;
John 25 50000
Alice 30 55000
Bob 22 48000
;
run;
* This is a single-line comment;
proc print data=employees;
run;
```

- **Summary**

SAS is a robust platform for performing complex data analyses and generating detailed reports.
Whether you are
managing large datasets,
performing predictive analytics, or
generating business insights, SAS provides the tools and flexibility needed for high-level data processing. Understanding the basic structure of SAS programming, the environment, and how it executes programs are foundational to mastering SAS.

In the following chapter , let us dive deeper into specific functionalities, including data manipulation, analysis procedures, and visualization techniques that will help you harness the full power of SAS.

CHAPTER TWO

Working with Data in SAS

In SAS, the ability to manage, manipulate, and analyze data is at the heart of its power. The **DATA Step** is one of the most important components of SAS, allowing you to read, create, and transform datasets. This chapter will delve into how to work with data in SAS, focusing on reading in data from various sources, creating new datasets, and applying essential data manipulation techniques.

- The DATA Step

The **DATA Step** is used in SAS to create and manipulate datasets. It reads data into SAS, applies transformations, and stores the results in a SAS dataset. A typical DATA Step consists of the following elements:

- **DATA Statement**: Defines the name of the dataset to be created or modified.
- **INPUT Statement**: Specifies the format in which the data is to be read.
- **DATALINES Statement**: Used to input raw data directly within the program.
- **RUN Statement**: Signals the end of the DATA Step.

Example:
data employees;
input Name $ Age Salary;
datalines;
John 30 55000
Alice 35 62000
Mark 28 50000
;
run;
In this example:

- The DATA statement creates a dataset called employees.

- The INPUT statement defines the variables Name, Age, and Salary with appropriate data types (e.g., $ indicates character variables).
- The DATALINES statement reads in raw data.
- The RUN statement completes the data step.

- Importing Data from External Sources

SAS is capable of importing data from a wide range of external sources, including text files (CSV, TXT), Excel spreadsheets, databases, and more. The PROC IMPORT procedure is often used to read data from external files.

- Importing a CSV File

You can import data from a CSV file using PROC IMPORT. Here's an example:

proc import datafile="C:\data\employees.csv"
out=employees
dbms=csv
replace;
getnames=yes;
run;

- DATAFILE specifies the location of the CSV file.
- OUT defines the name of the dataset to create.
- DBMS=csv tells SAS that the file format is CSV.
- REPLACE ensures that if the dataset already exists, it will be replaced.
- GETNAMES=YES tells SAS to use the first row of the file as variable names.

- Importing Excel Files

To import data from an Excel file, you use PROC IMPORT with DBMS=xlsx:

```
proc import datafile="C:\data\employees.xlsx"
out=employees
dbms=xlsx
replace;
sheet="Sheet1";
getnames=yes;
run;
```

- DBMS=xlsx specifies that the file is an Excel spreadsheet.
- SHEET tells SAS which sheet to import.

- Reading Data from Databases

SAS can also connect to external databases using SAS/ ACCESS. The LIBNAME statement allows you to connect to various database management systems (DBMS). For example, to connect to a MySQL database:

```
libname mydb mysql er="username"
password="password" database="dbname"
server="server_name";
proc print data=mydb.employees;
run;
```

In this case:

- The LIBNAME statement connects to the MySQL database.
- You can reference tables in the database as mydb.table_name in subsequent SAS steps.

- Data Types in SAS

Understanding data types is critical when working with datasets in SAS. There are two primary types of variables in SAS:

1. **Numeric**: Represents numbers, which can be used for mathematical operations. By default, numeric variables are stored as floating-point numbers.
2. **Character**: Represents text or string data. A character variable can store letters, numbers, and special characters but cannot be used in mathematical operations.

When defining variables in the INPUT statement, you use $ to denote a character variable. Numeric variables do not need any special notation.

Example:

```
data employees;
input Name $ Age Salary;
datalines;
John 30 55000
Alice 35 62000
;
run;
```

In this example, Name is a character variable (indicated by the $), and Age and Salary are numeric variables.

- Basic Data Manipulation

SAS provides a variety of tools for manipulating data in the DATA step. Some common tasks include creating new variables, modifying existing ones, and applying conditional logic.

- Creating New Variables

You can create new variables in the DATA step by assigning values to them.opy code

```
data employees;
set employees;
Bonus = Salary * 0.10;
run;
```

This example reads in the existing employees dataset, creates a new variable Bonus, and assigns it a value equal to 10% of Salary.

- Conditional Logic

SAS allows the use of conditional statements such as IF-THEN to apply logic based on specific conditions.

```
data employees;
set employees;
if Age > 30 then Seniority = "Senior";
else Seniority = "Junior";
run;
```

In this example, a new variable Seniority is created based on the condition that employees older than 30 are classified as "Senior" and others as "Junior".

- Subsetting Data

Subsetting is the process of selecting a portion of a dataset based on specific criteria. This can be done using the WHERE statement or conditional logic within the DATA step.

- **Using the WHERE Statement**

```
proc print data=employees;
where Age > 30;
run;
```

This example prints only the rows where the Age variable is greater than 30.

- **Using IF Statements in the DATA Step**

```
data senior_employees;
set employees;
if Age > 30;
run;
```

This example creates a new dataset senior_employees containing only employees older than 30.

- Merging Datasets

One of SAS's powerful features is its ability to merge datasets. The MERGE statement allows you to combine datasets based on common variables (often called **keys**).

- **Oneto-One Merging**

```
data combined;
merge employees departments;
by EmployeeID;
run;
```

In this example, the datasets employees and departments are merged by the common variable EmployeeID.

- **Oneto-Many Merging**

```
data full_data;
merge employees projects;
```

by EmployeeID;

run;

When one dataset has multiple rows for a single EmployeeID (as in the case of multiple projects), SAS will still merge on the common variable, keeping all relevant rows.

- Sorting Data

SAS provides the PROC SORT procedure for sorting datasets by one or more variables.

proc sort data=employees;

by Salary;

run;

This example sorts the employees dataset by the Salary variable in ascending order.

To sort in descending order:

proc sort data=employees;

by descending Salary;

run;

- Saving and Exporting Data

Once you've manipulated your data, you may want to save it to disk or export it to a different format for use in other programs.

- **Saving SAS Datasets**

You can save SAS datasets to a specific location using the LIBNAME statement.

libname mylib 'C:\sasdata';

data mylib.employees;

set employees;

run;

This code saves the employees dataset to the folder C:\sasdata under the library mylib.

- **Exporting to CSV**

To export a dataset to a CSV file, you can use the PROC EXPORT procedure.

```
proc export data=employees
outfile="C:\data\employees.csv"
dbms=csv
replace;
run;
```

This example exports the employees dataset to a CSV file.

- **Summary**

This chapter provided an introduction to working with data in SAS, focusing on importing and exporting datasets, basic data manipulation, subsetting, and merging datasets. SAS's powerful data handling capabilities allow for flexible and efficient processing of large datasets, making it an invaluable tool for data-driven decision-making.

This chapter provided an introduction to working with data in SAS, focusing on importing and exporting datasets, basic data manipulation, subsetting, and merging datasets. SAS's powerful data handling capabilities allow for flexible and efficient processing of large datasets, making it an invaluable tool for data-driven decision-making. In the next chapter, we will explore more advanced data manipulation techniques and the use of **PROC** steps to analyze and report on data.

CHAPTER THREE

Advanced Data Manipulation Techniques

In this chapter, we will explore more advanced techniques for managing and manipulating data in SAS. You'll learn about functions, arrays, and additional data-handling techniques that can improve efficiency and simplify complex data processing tasks. Understanding and applying these advanced concepts will make you more adept at managing large datasets and performing sophisticated transformations.

- SAS Functions

SAS provides a rich library of built-in **functions** for performing a wide range of operations, including mathematical calculations, character manipulations, and date/time handling. Functions make your code more efficient and eliminate the need for writing complex logic from scratch.

- Numeric Functions

Numeric functions perform operations on numeric variables. Some commonly used numeric functions include:

- **SUM**: Adds values together. If any value is missing, it ignores that value.

```
data employees;
set employees;
TotalSalary = sum(Salary, Bonus);
run;
```

- **ROUND**: Rounds a number to a specified number of decimal places.

```
data rounded_salaries;
set employees;
RoundedSalary = round(Salary, 1000);
run;
```

- **MEAN**: Calculates the average of numeric variables.

```
data employees;
set employees;
AvgPay = mean(Salary, Bonus);
run;
```

- **Character Functions**

- Character functions operate on string (character) data. Some commonly used character functions include:

- **UPCASE**: Converts a character string to uppercase.

```
data employees;
set employees;
NameUpper = upcase(Name);
run;
```

- **SUBSTR**: Extracts a portion of a string.

```
data employees;
set employees;
FirstInitial = substr(Name, 1, 1);
run;
```

- **CAT**: Concatenates two or more strings together.

```
data employees;
set employees;
FullName = cat(Name, ' ', Surname);
run;
```

- **Date Functions**

SAS stores dates as the number of days since January 1, 1960. Date functions allow you to manipulate and format date variables effectively.

- **TODAY**: Returns the current date.

```
data employees;
set employees;
CurrentDate = today();
run;
```

- **INTCK**: Calculates the difference between two dates in specified units (e.g., days, months, years).

```
data employees;
set employees;
YearsOfService = intck('year', HireDate, today());
```

run;

CHAPTER FOUR

Statistical Analysis and Reporting in SAS

SAS excels in statistical analysis, offering a comprehensive suite of procedures and tools for performing descriptive statistics, hypothesis testing, regression, and more. This chapter will cover how to conduct statistical analysis and create detailed reports in SAS. We'll explore key procedures such as PROC MEANS, PROC FREQ, PROC UNIVARIATE, and regression techniques, alongside generating effective reports using the ODS system.

Descriptive Statistics

Descriptive statistics provide simple summaries about the data, such as mean, median, mode, variance, and standard deviation. SAS provides several procedures to perform these tasks.

- **PROC MEANS**

PROC MEANS generates basic descriptive statistics, such as the mean, standard deviation, and sum, for numeric variables.

```
proc means data=employees mean median std min max;
var Salary Age;
```

run;

- The VAR statement specifies which variables to calculate statistics for (Salary and Age in this case).
- Common statistics like mean, median, standard deviation (std), minimum (min), and maximum (max) can be specified.

- **PROC SUMMARY**

PROC SUMMARY is very similar to PROC MEANS, but with more flexible options for producing customized output.

```
proc summary data=employees;
var Salary Age;
output    out=summary_data    mean=MeanSalary MeanAge;
run;
```

- The output statement creates a new dataset (summary_data) containing the calculated means of Salary and Age.

- **PROC UNIVARIATE**

PROC UNIVARIATE provides more detailed descriptive statistics, including measures of skewness, kurtosis, and tests for normality.

```
proc univariate data=employees;
var Salary;
histogram Salary;
run;
```

- The HISTOGRAM statement generates a histogram of the Salary variable, and PROC UNIVARIATE provides statistics like skewness, kurtosis, and normality tests.

Frequency Analysis

Frequency analysis provides a count of occurrences for each value of a categorical variable. This can be useful for understanding the distribution of categories within your data.

- **PROC FREQ**

PROC FREQ generates frequency tables and can also compute percentages and cumulative percentages.

```
proc freq data=employees;
tables Department JobTitle;
run;
```

- The tables statement specifies the variables (Department and JobTitle) for which frequency distributions will be calculated.

- **CrossTabulation with PROC FREQ**

You can generate two-way or multi-way cross-tabulations to analyze the relationship between two or more categorical variables.

```
proc freq data=employees;
tables Department*Gender / chisq;
run;
```

- The Department*Gender statement generates a cross-tabulation of these two variables.

- The /chisq option performs a chi-square test of independence to determine whether there is a significant association between the variables.

- **Correlation and Regression Analysis**

SAS offers powerful tools for correlation and regression analysis to help identify relationships between variables.

- **Correlation with PROC CORR**

PROC CORR calculates correlation coefficients, which measure the strength of the linear relationship between variables.

```
proc corr data=employees;
var Age Salary;
run;
```

This example calculates the Pearson correlation coefficient between Age and Salary.

- **Simple Linear Regression with PROC REG**

Linear regression models the relationship between a dependent variable and one or more independent variables. PROC REG is used for simple and multiple linear regression.

```
proc reg data=employees;
model Salary = Age;
run;
quit;
```

- The model statement specifies Salary as the dependent variable and Age as the independent variable.

- PROC REG outputs parameter estimates, confidence intervals, and diagnostics for the regression model.

- **Multiple Linear Regression**

Multiple linear regression is used when there are multiple independent variables predicting the dependent variable.

```
proc reg data=employees;
model Salary = Age Experience Education;
run;
quit;
```

In this example, Salary is modeled as a function of Age, Experience, and Education. The procedure provides insights into the contribution of each predictor.

- **Hypothesis Testing**

SAS supports a wide variety of statistical tests for hypothesis testing, such as t-tests, ANOVA, and chi-square tests.

- **Test with PROC TTEST**

The t-test compares the means of two groups to determine if they are significantly different.

```
proc ttest data=employees;
class Gender;
var Salary;
run;
```

- The class statement specifies the grouping variable (Gender).
- The var statement specifies the variable to compare across the groups (Salary).

- SAS will conduct a two-sample t-test to assess whether the mean Salary differs by Gender.

- **ANOVA with PROC ANOVA**

Analysis of variance (ANOVA) is used to compare the means of three or more groups.

```
proc anova data=employees;
class Department;
model Salary = Department;
run;
quit;
```

- The class statement specifies the categorical variable (Department).
- The model statement indicates that Salary is to be modeled based on the Department variable.

- **ChiSquare Test with PROC FREQ**

A chi-square test is used to assess the association between two categorical variables.

```
proc freq data=employees;
tables Gender*Department / chisq;
run;
```

This example performs a chi-square test to determine if there is a significant association between Gender and Department.

- **Generating Reports Using ODS (Output Delivery System)**

SAS's **Output Delivery System (ODS)** allows you to control the format and style of your output, sending results to various formats like HTML, PDF, RTF, or Excel.

- **Basic ODS Example**

To generate output in different formats, you use the ODS statements:

```
ods html file="C:\reports\report.html";
proc means data=employees;
var Salary;
run;
ods html close;
```

- The ods html statement directs output to an HTML file.
- ods html close closes the HTML destination after the PROC MEANS procedure.

- **Generating a PDF Report**

To create a PDF report:

```
ods pdf file="C:\reports\salary_report.pdf";
proc freq data=employees;
tables Department;
run;
ods pdf close;
```

In this example, the output of the PROC FREQ procedure is saved in a PDF file.

- **Creating an Excel Report**

SAS can also export output to Excel using the ods excel statement.

```
ods excel file="C:\reports\employee_data.xlsx";
proc print data=employees;
run;
ods excel close;
```

- The ods excel statement directs output to an Excel file.
- This example exports the employees dataset to an Excel spreadsheet.

- Customizing Output with ODS Styles

SAS allows you to customize the appearance of reports by applying different styles to your output.

```
ods        html        file="C:\reports\styled_report.html"
style=statistical;
    proc means data=employees;
    var Salary;
    run;
    ods html close;
```

In this example, the style=statistical option applies a pre-defined style to the output. SAS provides several built-in styles, such as statistical, journal, and htmlblue.

- Creating Graphs and Visualizations

SAS offers several procedures for generating graphs and visualizations, including histograms, bar charts, and scatter plots.

- **PROC SGPLOT**

PROC SGPLOT is used to create various types of graphs. Here's how to create a scatter plot:

```
    proc sgplot data=employees;
    scatter x=Age y=Salary;
    run;
```

This example plots Age on the x-axis and Salary on the y-axis.

- **Generating a Bar Chart**

```
proc sgplot data=employees;
vbar Department;
run;
```

This example generates a vertical bar chart showing the distribution of employees across departments.

- Summary

This chapter introduced statistical analysis and reporting techniques in SAS. We explored how to perform descriptive statistics, hypothesis testing, correlation, regression analysis, and ANOVA. Additionally, you learned how to generate and customize reports using the Output Delivery System (ODS). In the next chapter, we will dive into time series analysis and forecasting, where we will explore specialized procedures for analyzing temporal data.c

Chapter 5: Time Series An

Time Series Analysis and Forecasting in SAS

Time series analysis focuses on analyzing data points collected or recorded at specific time intervals. Understanding time series data and making forecasts based on this data is crucial in many fields, such as finance, economics, and business. In this chapter, we will introduce time series concepts, discuss data preparation techniques, and explore the powerful tools SAS offers for time series analysis and forecasting, such as PROC TIMESERIES, PROC ARIMA, and PROC FORECAST.

- Introduction to Time Series Data

Time series data consists of observations that are collected at successive points in time, usually at equally spaced intervals, such as daily, weekly, or monthly data. Each observation in a time series is influenced by time-dependent factors.

Key characteristics of time series data include:

- **Trend**: A long-term increase or decrease in the data.
- **Seasonality**: Regular, repeating fluctuations in data related to calendar events, such as monthly sales spikes.

- **Cyclical patterns**: Non-seasonal patterns that repeat over a longer time span, often linked to economic cycles.
- **Noise**: Random variability in the data that cannot be explained by the model.

- Preparing Time Series Data in SAS

Before performing time series analysis, it's essential to prepare the data properly. This includes sorting data by time, creating time indices, and handling missing values.

- Sorting Time Series Data

The first step is to ensure that the data is ordered chronologically. Use PROC SORT to sort your dataset by the time variable.

```
proc sort data=sales;
by Date;
run;
```

In this example, the sales data is sorted by the Date variable.

- Handling Missing Data

Missing data can be problematic in time series analysis. SAS provides several techniques to handle missing values, such as interpolation and carrying forward previous values.

```
data sales_filled;
set sales;
retain PrevValue;
if missing(Sales) then Sales = PrevValue; /* Carry forward previous value */
else PrevValue = Sales;
run;
```

Alternatively, you can use PROC EXPAND to perform interpolation:

```
proc expand data=sales out=sales_interp method=join;
id Date;
```

convert Sales;
run;
This example interpolates missing values for Sales using the method=join option in PROC EXPAND.

- Time Series Analysis with PROC TIMESERIES

PROC TIMESERIES is a powerful procedure for basic time series analysis and data manipulation. It allows you to transform time series data, calculate descriptive statistics, and identify trends and seasonality.

- **Basic Time Series Analysis**

  proc timcseries data=sales out=stats;
  id Date interval=month;
  var Sales;
  run;
  In this example:
  The id sta
  In this example:

- The id statement defines the time variable (Date) and the interval (month).
- The var statement specifies the variable to analyze (Sales).

- **Decomposing Time Series Components**

  You can use PROC TIMESERIES to decompose a time series into its components: trend, seasonality, and residual noise.

  proc timeseries data=sales outdecomp=decomposed;
  id Date interval=month;
  var Sales;

```
decomp mode=additive; /* Additive decomposition */
run;
```

The decomp statement specifies the decomposition model. In this case, we are using an additive model, which assumes the components add up to the observed data.

- Forecasting with PROC FORECAST

PROC FORECAST is used to generate forecasts based on time series data. This procedure can handle trend and seasonality while forecasting future values.

- **Basic Forecasting**

```
proc forecast data=sales out=forecast lead=12 interval=month;
    id Date;
    var Sales;
    run;
```

In this example:

The lead=12 option tells SAS to generate forecasts for the next 12 months.

The lead=12 option tells SAS to generate forecasts for the next 12 months.

The interval=month option specifies the time interval.

- **Adjusting for Seasonality**

To improve forecast accuracy, you can account for seasonality by specifying the seasonal cycle.

```
proc forecast data=sales out=forecast lead=12 interval=month season=12;
    id Date;
    var Sales;
    run;
```

In this example, the season=12 option adjusts for a yearly cycle (12 months).

- **Plotting the Forecast**

  You can visualize the forecast using PROC SGPLOT:
  proc sgplot data=forecast;
  series x=Date y=Sales / lineattrs=(color=blue);
  series x=Date y=Forecast / lineattrs=(color=red);
  run;
  In this example:
  The first series statement plots the actual sales data.
  The second series statement plots the forecast values.
  - **ARIMA Modeling with PROC ARIMA**

- Autoregressive Integrated Moving Average (ARIMA) models are widely used in time series analysis for modeling and forecasting. PROC ARIMA allows you to fit ARIMA models to time series data, test model assumptions, and generate forecasts.
- **Fitting an ARIMA Model**

  To fit an ARIMA model, you need to identify the autoregressive (AR), differencing (I), and moving average (MA) components.
  proc arima data=sales;
  identify var=Sales;
  estimate p=1 q=1;
  forecast lead=12 out=forecast_arima;
  run;
  In this example:

- The identify statement specifies the variable to mod

```
proc arima data=sales;
identify var=Sales;
estimate p=1 q=1;
forecast lead=12 out=forecast_arima;
residuals plot;
run;
```

The residuals plot option generates a plot of residuals, helping you assess the fit of the ARIMA model.

- Exponential Smoothing with PROC ESM

Exponential smoothing is another popular technique for time series forecasting. It assigns exponentially decreasing weights to past observations, making it useful for data with trends and seasonality.

- **Simple Exponential Smoothing**

```
proc esm data=sales out=forecast_esm lead=12;
id Date interval=month;
forecast Sales / model=simple;
run;
```

This example uses simple exponential smoothing to forecast future values of Sales.

Holt-Winters Model

The Holt-Winters model is an extension of exponential smoothing that handles both trends and seasonality.

```
proc esm data=sales out=forecast_hw lead=12;
id Date interval=month;
forecast Sales / model=addwinters;
run;
```

The addwinters option specifies an additive Holt-Winters model, which is ideal for time series with both trend and seasonality components.

- Advanced Time Series Techniques

SAS offers several other procedures for advanced time series analysis, such as state space modeling and spectral analysis.

- **State Space Models with PROC SSM**

State space models allow for the analysis of complex, dynamic systems, such as financial markets or weather patterns.

```
proc ssm data=sales;
id Date interval=month;
model Sales = (trend cycle);
run;
```

In this example, a state space model is applied to analyze the Saldata using both a trend and a cyclical component.

- **Spectral Analysis with PROC SPECTRA**
- Spectral analysis is used to examine the frequency components of a time series.

```
proc spectra data=sales;
var Sales;
run;
```

PROC SPECTRA performs a frequency-domain analysis of the time series data, providing insights into cyclical patterns that may not be apparent in the time domain.

- **Generating Reports for Time Series Analysis**

After performing time series analysis, generating a clear and concise report is essential. Use the Output Delivery System (ODS) to create reports in formats such as PDF, HTML, and Excel.

- **PDF Report Example**

```
ods pdf file="C:\reports\time_series_report.pdf";
proc forecast data=sales out=forecast lead=12;
id Date;
var Sales;
run;
ods pdf close;
```

This example generates a PDF report that includes the forecasted time series.

- **Excel Report Example**

```
ods excel file="C:\reports\time_series_report.xlsx";
proc arima data=sales;
identify var=Sales;
estimate p=1 q=1;
forecast lead=12 out=forecast_arima;
run;
ods excel close;
```

Here, the ARIMA analysis and forecast are exported to an Excel report.

Time series analysis involves analyzing data collected at regular intervals over time. It's crucial for understanding trends, seasonal patterns, and making predictions. This chapter will explore time series concepts, data preparation, and methods for analyzing and forecasting time series using SAS. We will use procedures such as PROC TIMESERIES, PROC FORECAST, and PROC ARIMA to develop models and generate forecasts.

- **Introduction to Time Series Data**

Time series data refers to observations made at specific time intervals, such as daily, monthly, or yearly. Common patterns in time series data include:

Trend: The long-term increase or decrease in the data.

Seasonality: Regular, repeating patterns in the data, usually tied to calendar-based cycles, such as higher sales during holidays.

Cyclic patterns: Fluctuations that are not tied to a specific time frame, often related to economic or business cycles.

Noise: Random fluctuations that cannot be explained by the model.

Preparing Time Series Data for Analysis

Before analyzing time series data, it must be prepared properly. This includes sorting the data by time, handling missing values, and creating appropriate time intervals.

- **Sorting Data by Time**

- The first step in time series analysis is to ensure that the data is sorted by time. Use PROC SORT to arrange the dataset by the time variable.

  ```
  proc sort data=sales;
  by Date;
  run;
  ```

  This ensures the data is ordered by the Date variable, which is crucial for accurate time series analysis.

- **Handling Missing Values**

- Time series data often contains missing values, which can distort analysis. SAS offers several ways to handle missing data, such as filling missing values with previous values or using interpolation.

```
data sales_clean;
set sales;
retain LastValue;
if missing(Sales) then Sales = LastValue; /* Carry forward previous value */
else LastValue = Sales;
run;
```

Alternatively, use PROC EXPAND for more sophisticated interpolation methods:

```
proc expand data=sales out=sales_interp method=join;
id Date;
convert Sales;
run;
```

This interpolates the missing values for the Sales variable using the join method.

- **Basic Time Series Analysis with PROC TIMESERIES**

PROC TIMESERIES is a versatile tool for analyzing time series data. It can compute descriptive statistics, identify trends, and perform seasonal adjustments.

- **Calculating Statistics with PROC TIMESERIES**
- proc timeseries data=sales out=stats;

```
id Date interval=month;
var Sales;
run;
```

In this example:
- The id statement defines Date as the time variable and sets the interval to month.
- The var statement specifies the variable to analyze (Sales).
- **Decomposing Time Series**

- You can decompose a time series into its trend, seasonal, and residual components using PROC TIMESERIES.

    proc timeseries data=sales outdecomp=decomposed;
    id Date interval=month;
    var Sales;
    decomp mode=additive; /* Additive decomposition */
    run;

    The decomp statement specifies that an additive model will be used to break down the time series.

- **- Forecasting Time Series Data with PROC FORECAST**

PROC FORECAST is a simple yet powerful tool for generating forecasts based on time series data.

- Basic Forecasting Example

    proc forecast data=sales out=forecast lead=12 interval=month;
    id Date;
    var Sales;
    run;

In this example:

The lead=12 option forecasts 12 periods (months) into the future.

The interval=month option specifies that the data is monthly.

- Seasonal Adjustment in Forecasting

To account for seasonality, specify the seasonal cycle in your forecast.

    proc forecast data=sales out=forecast lead=12 interval=month season=12;
    id Date;
    var Sales;
    run;

Here, the season=12 option adjusts for yearly seasonality (12 months).

- **Plotting the Forecast**

- Use PROC SGPLOT to visualize the forecasted results:

```
proc sgplot data=forecast;
series x=Date y=Sales / lineattrs=(color=blue);
series x=Date y=Forecast / lineattrs=(color=red);
run;
```

This example plots both actual and forecasted sales data.

- **Advanced Forecasting with PROC ARIMA**
- PROC ARIMA is used to fit ARIMA models, which are particularly useful for time series data with trends and autocorrelation. The ARIMA model has three components:
- **AR (Autoregressive)**: The relationship between the current value and its previous values.
- **I (Integrated)**: Differencing the data to remove trends.
- **MA (Moving Average)**: The relationship between the current value and past forecast errors.
- **Fitting an ARIMA Model**
- sas

```
Copy code
proc arima data=sales;
identify var=Sales;
estimate p=1 q=1;
forecast lead=12 out=forecast_arima;
run;
```

In this example:

The identify statement specifies the variable to model (Sales).

The estimate statement fits an ARIMA(1,1,1) model, where p=1 is the autoregressive term, and q=1 is the moving average term.

The forecast statement generates forecasts for 12 periods.

Checking Residuals

- It's important to check the residuals to ensure that the model fits well.

```
proc arima data=sales;
identify var=Sales;
estimate p=1 q=1;
forecast lead=12 out=forecast_arima;
residuals plot;
run;
```

This produces a plot of the residuals to assess model accuracy.

- Exponential Smoothing with PROC ESM

Exponential smoothing methods assign exponentially decreasing weights to past observations. SAS provides simple, double, and Holt-Winters exponential smoothing techniques.

- **Simple Exponential Smoothing**

```
proc esm data=sales out=forecast_esm lead=12;
id Date interval=month;
forecast Sales / model=simple;
run;
```

This method smooths out data using simple exponential smoothing.

- **HoltWinters Seasonal Model**

The Holt-Winters method handles both trend and seasonality.

```
proc esm data=sales out=forecast_hw lead=12;
id Date interval=month;
forecast Sales / model=addwinters;
run;
```

Here, the addwinters option specifies the additive Holt-Winters model.

- **Advanced Time Series Techniques**

- **State Space Models with PROC SSM**

State space models are useful for modeling dynamic systems with unobservable states.

```
proc ssm data=sales;
id Date interval=month;
model Sales = (trend cycle);
run;
```

This model includes both a trend and a cyclical component.

- **Analysis with PROC SPECTRA**
- Spectral analysis is used to study the frequency components of a time series.

```
proc spectra data=sales;
var Sales;
run;
```

PROC SPECTRA helps identify periodic patterns in the data.

- **Generating Reports with ODS**

- After performing analysis, you can use the Output Delivery System (ODS) to generate reports in various formats, such as PDF and Excel.
- **PDF Report Example**
- ods pdf file="C:\reports\time_series_report.pdf";
    proc forecast data=sales out=forecast lead=12;
    id Date;
    var Sales;
    run;
    ods pdf close;
    This generates a PDF report with the forecasted results.

- **Excel Report Example**

ods excel file="C:\reports\time_series_report.xlsx";
proc arima data=sales;
identify var=Sales;
estimate p=1 q=1;
forecast lead=12 out=forecast_arima;
run;
ods excel close;

This exports the ARIMA forecast to an Excel spreadsheet.

- **Summary**

In this chapter, we explored the fundamentals of time series analysis, including data preparation, basic and advanced forecasting techniques, and model diagnostics. We examined methods such as ARIMA, exponential smoothing, and state space models for forecasting. You also learned how to use the Output Delivery System to generate time series reports. In the next chapter, we will focus on survival analysis and its applications using SAS.

el (Sales).
- The estimate statement fits an ARIMA(1,1,1) model, meaning one autoregressive term (p=1), one differencing term (I), and one moving average term (q=1).
- The forecast statement generates forecasts for the next 12 periods.

- Checking Residuals

- It's essential to check the residuals to ensure that the model fits the data well.

```
proc arima data=sales;
identify var=Sales;
estimate p=1 q=1;
forecast lead=12 out=forecast_arima;
```

Epilogue

As we close this journey through the essentials and complexities of SAS programming, it's essential to reflect on the transformative potential this skill set can offer.

From data wrangling to statistical analysis, from reporting to advanced analytics, SAS opens doors to a more profound understanding of data and empowers you to bring clarity to the seemingly chaotic information we encounter daily.

Mastery, as discussed throughout this book, is a process—not a destination.

The techniques, best practices, and hands-on exercises you've explored in these chapters are a solid foundation, but they are just the beginning.

The field of data analytics continues to evolve at a rapid pace, and the SAS ecosystem evolves with it. Staying proficient means continuously experimenting with new functionalities, exploring other SAS modules, and expanding your toolkit with fresh techniques and strategies.

As you continue to analyze, interpret, and communicate data-driven insights, remember that the ultimate goal is to tell compelling, accurate, and actionable stories with data. In doing so, you have the power to shape decisions, drive innovation, and contribute meaningfully to any field you apply your expertise to—whether it's business, health, social sciences, or beyond.

Thank you for allowing this book to be part of your learning journey.

May your path in SAS programming be one of discovery, growth, and impactful analysis.

Happy coding, and best wishes for your journey to mastering SAS!